Easy Classical Violin & Piano Duets

Featuring music of Bach, Mozart, Beethoven, Strauss and other composers.

Easy Classical Violin & Piano Duets
Revised Edition

© Javier Marcó

ISBN-13:978-1466307933
ISBN-10:1466307935

Contents

Playing guide 5

1812 Overture, Op. 49. 11

An der schönen blauen Donau, Op. 314 12

Bourrée, BWV 996 14

Dance of the Flowers, Op. 71a 16

Eine kleine Nachtmusik, K.525 18

Für Elise, WoO 59 20

Greensleeves 22

Guten Abend, gut' Nacht 24

I Dovregubbens hall 26

Jesus bleibet meine Freude, BWV 147 28

Kanon in D-Dur 30

La Donna è Mobile 32

la Primavera, RV. 269 34

Menuett, BWV Anh 114 36

Ode an die Freude, Op. 125 38

Pomp and Circumstance March N°1, Op. 39 .40

Treulich geführt 42

Water Music, HWV 349 44

Playing guide

Standard notation
Notes are written on a Staff.

Staff
The staff consists of five lines and four spaces, on which notes symbols are placed.

Clef
A clef assigns an individual note to a certain line.

The **Treble Clef** or **G Clef** is used for the violin.

This clef indicates the position of the note G which is on the second line from the bottom.

Note
A note is a sign used to represent the relative pitch of a sound.

There are seven notes: A, B, C, D, E, F and G.

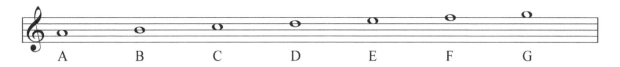

Ledger lines
The ledger lines are used to inscribe notes outside the lines and spaces of the staff.

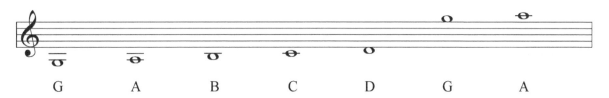

Accidentals

An accidental is a symbol to raise or lower the pitch of a note.

♯ sharp   Next note up half step.

♭ flat   Next note down half step.

♮ natural   Cancels a flat or a sharp.

Note values

A **note value** is used to indicate the duration of a note. A **rest** is an interval of silence, marked by a sign indicating the length of the pause. Each rest corresponds to a particular note value.

𝅝	Whole note	𝄻	Whole rest
𝅗𝅥	Half note	𝄼	Half rest
𝅘𝅥	Quarter note	𝄽	Quarter rest
𝅘𝅥𝅮	Eighth note	𝄾	Eighth rest
𝅘𝅥𝅯	Sixteenth note	𝄿	Sixteenth rest

Dotted note

A dotted note is a note with a small dot written after it. The dot adds half as much again to the basic note's duration.

Tie

A tie is a curved line connecting the heads of two notes of the same pitch, indicating that they are to be played as a single note with a duration equal to the sum of the individual notes' note values.

Bars or Measures

The staff is divided into equal segments of time consisting of the same number of beats, called bar or measures.

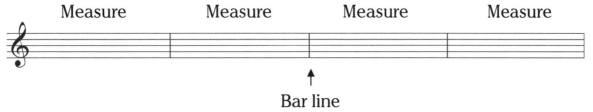

Bar line

Time signature

Time signature consists of two numbers, the upper number specifies how many beats (or counts) are in each measure, and the lower number tells us the note value which represents one beat.

Example: 4/4 means four quarters, or four beats per measure with a quarter note receiving one beat or count.

Key signature

A Key signature is a group of accidentals, generally written at the beginning of a score immediately after the clef, and shows which notes always get sharps or flats. Accidentals on the lines and spaces in the key signature affect those notes throughout the piece unless there is a natural sign.

Repeat sign

The repeat sign indicates a section should be repeated from the beginning, and then continue on. A corresponding sign facing the other way indicates where the repeat is to begin.

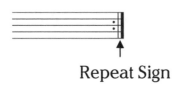

Repeat Sign

First and second endings
The section should be repeated from the beginning, and number brackets above the bars indicate which to played the first time (1), which to play the second time (2).

Dynamics
Dynamics refers to the volume of the notes.

p (piano), meaning soft.
mp (mezzo-piano), meaning "moderately soft".
mf (mezzo-forte), meaning "moderately loud".
f (forte), meaning loud.

————————— **Crescendo**. A gradual increase in volume.

————————— **Decrescendo**. A gradual decrease in volume.

Tempo Markings
Tempo is written at the beginning of a piece of music and indicates how slow or fast this piece should be played.

Lento — very slow (40–60 bpm)
Adagio — slow and stately (66–76 bpm)
Andate — at a walking pace (76–108 bpm)
Moderato — moderately (101-110 bpm)
Allegretto — moderately fast (but less so than allegro)
Allegro — fast, quickly and bright (120–139 bpm)
Presto — extremely fast (180–200 bpm)

Alla marcia — in the manner of a march
In tempo di valse — in tempo of vals

rallentando — gradual slowing down
a tempo — returns to the base tempo after a *rallentando*

Articulation

Legato. Notes are played smoothly and connected.

Stacatto. Notes are played separated or detached from its neighbours by a silence.

Fermata (pause)
The note is to be prolonged at the pleasure of the performer.

Fingering
In this book left hand fingering is indicated using numbers above the staff.
0= open
1= index
2= middle
3= ring
4= little finger

Bowings

Down-bow   Up-bow

Slur
Indicates that two or more notes are to be played in one bow.

1 8 1 2 ГОД, Op. 49

(1812 Overture)

Piotr Ilyich Tchaikovsky

11

An der schönen blauen Donau, Op. 314

Johann Strauss II

In Tempo di Valse

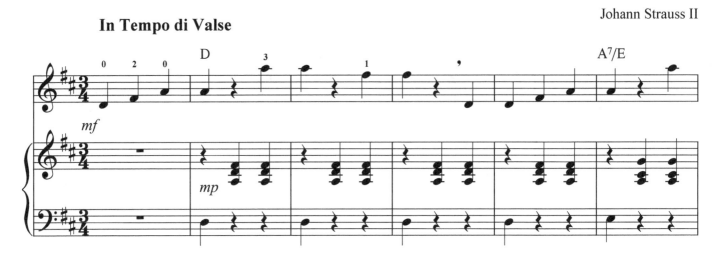

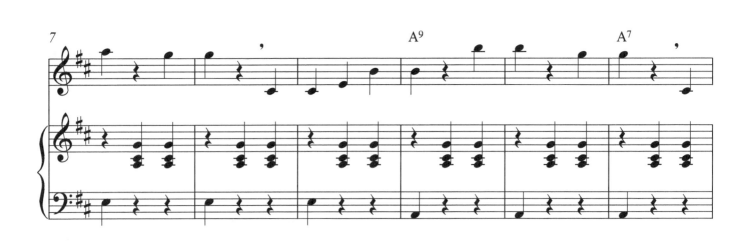

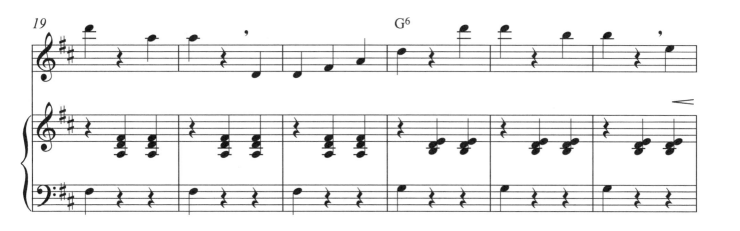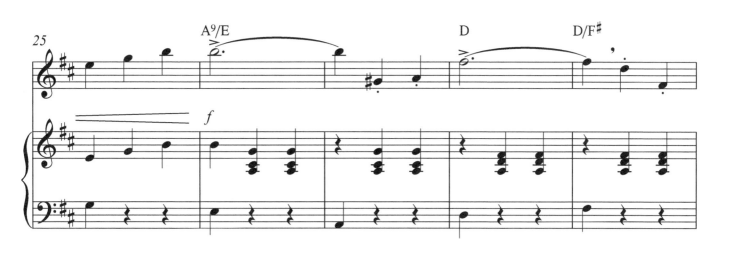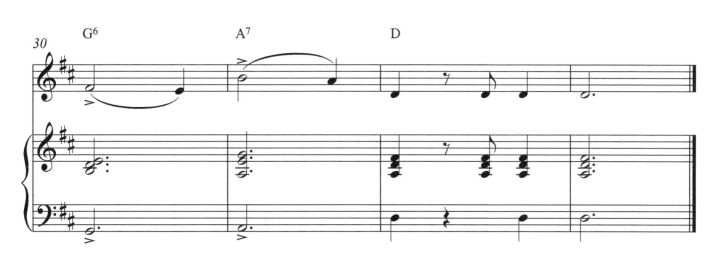

Bourrée, BWV 996

Johann Sebastian Bach

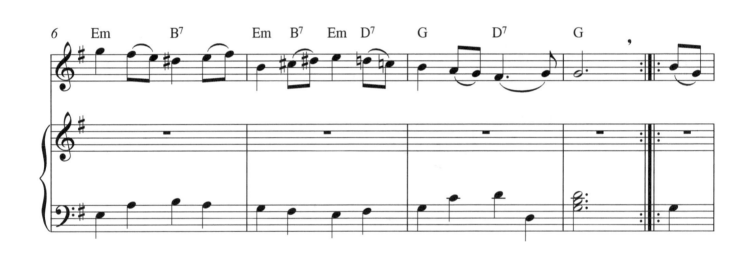
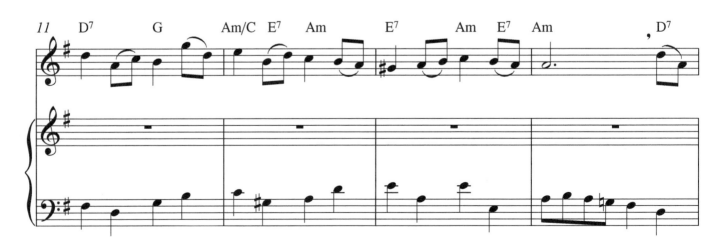

Щелкунчик, Op. 71a

(Dance of the Flowers)

Piotr Ilyich Tchaikovsky

Tempo di Valse

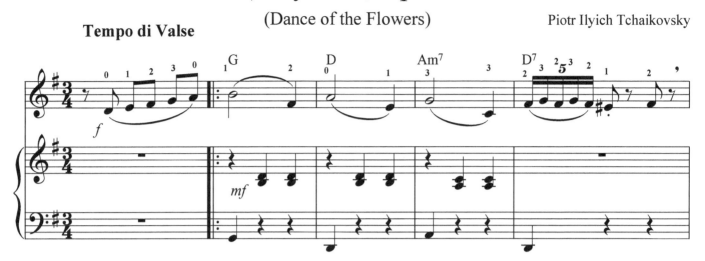

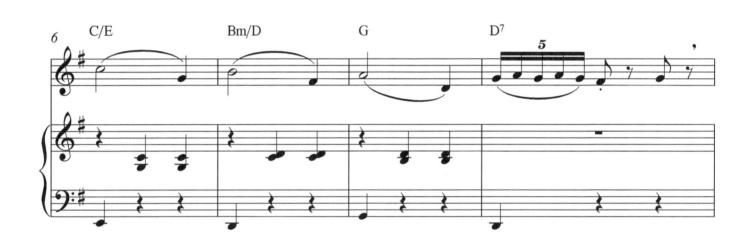

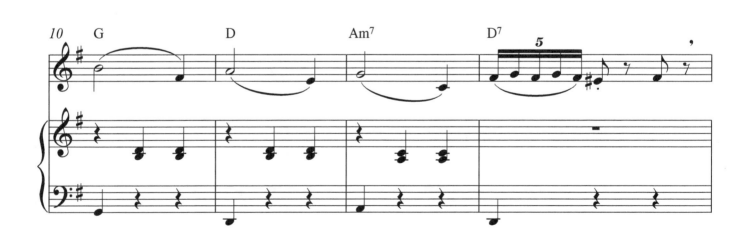

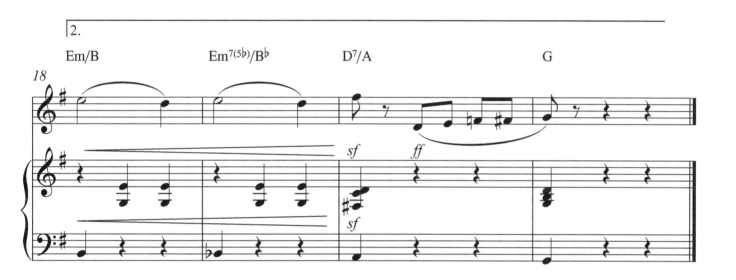

Eine kleine Nachtmusik, K.525

Wolfgang Amadeus Mozart

Allegro

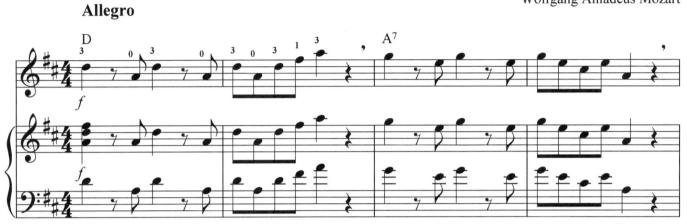

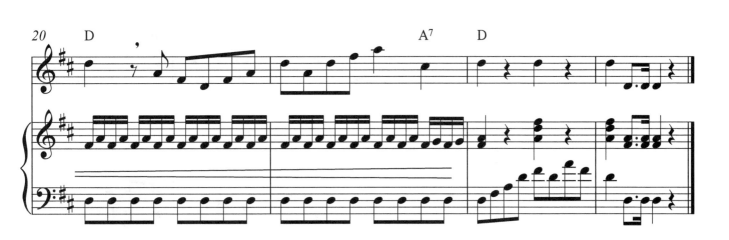

Für Elise, WoO 59

Ludwig van Beethoven

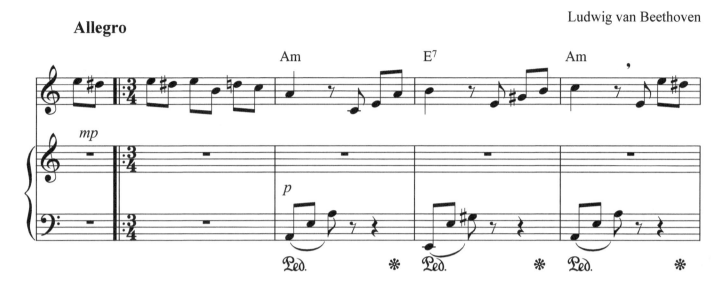
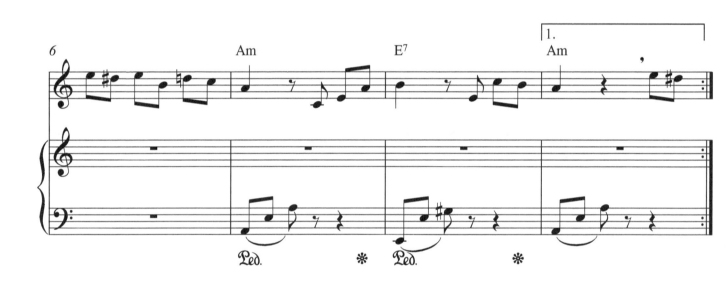
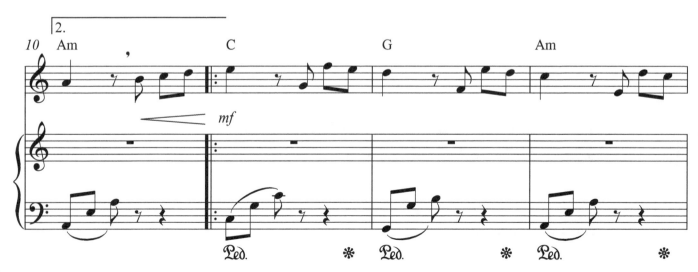

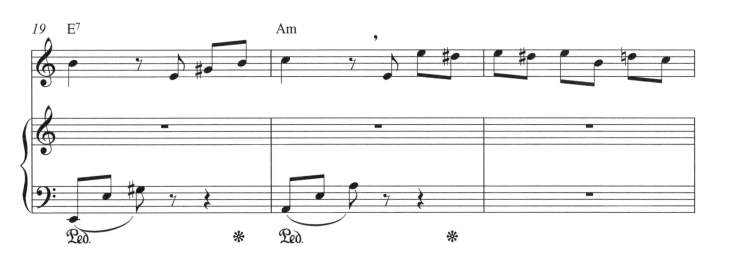

Greensleeves

Traditional English Folk Song

Guten Abend, gut' Nacht

Johannes Brahms

I Dovregubbens hall

Edvard Grieg

Jesus bleibet meine Freude, BWV 147

Johann Sebastian Bach

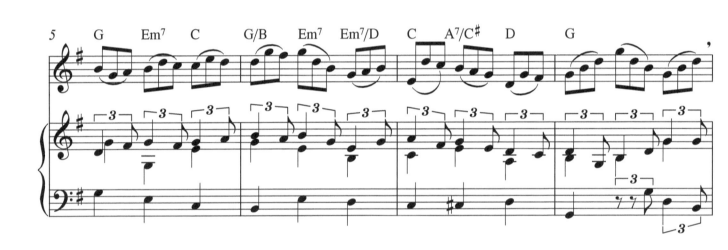

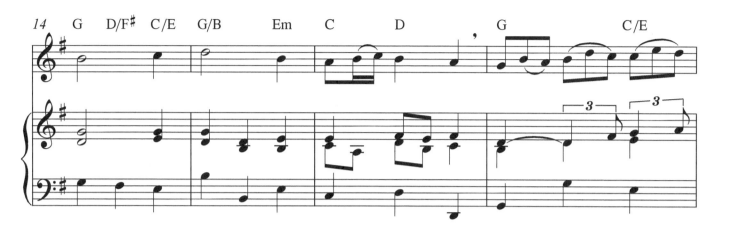
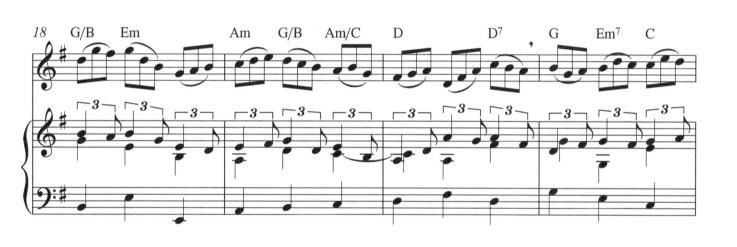
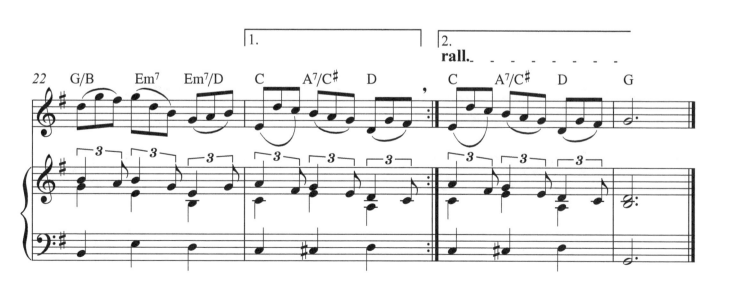

Kanon in D-Dur

Johann Pachelbel

Adagio

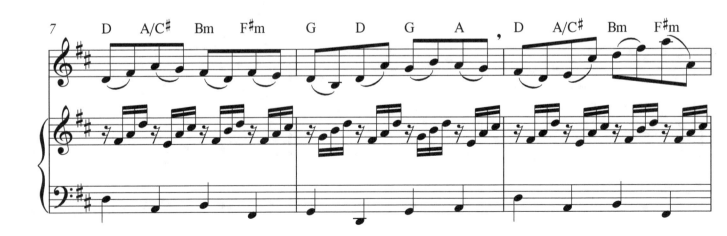

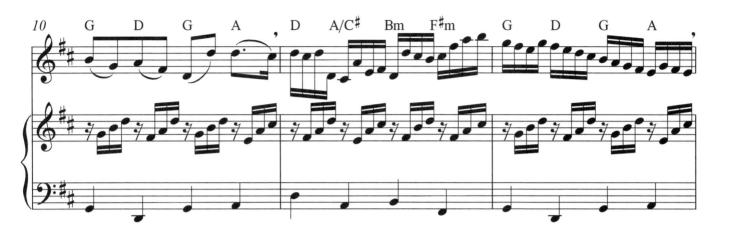

La Donna è Mobile

Giuseppe Verdi

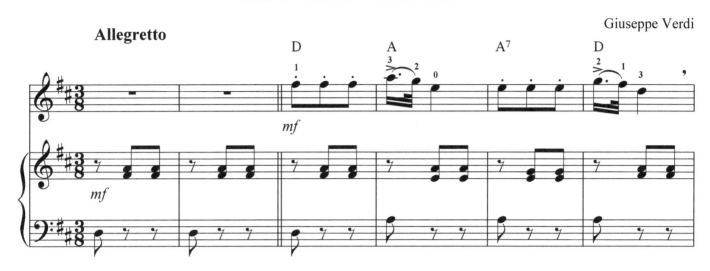
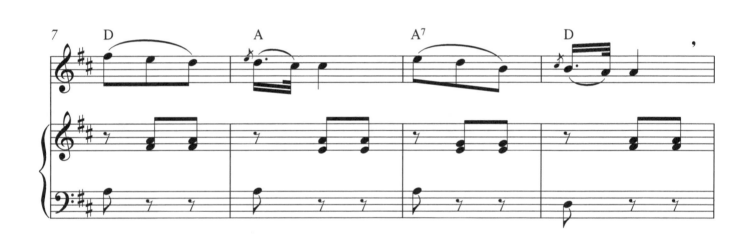
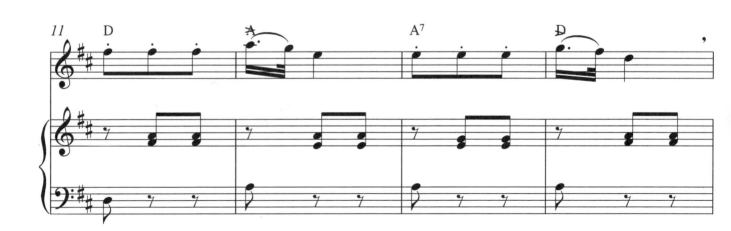

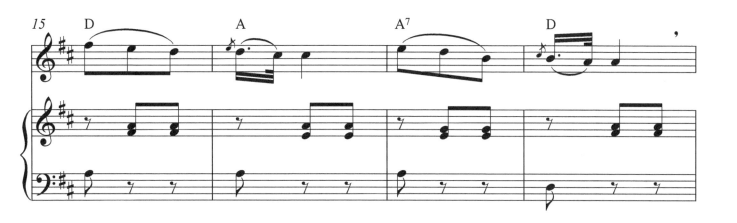

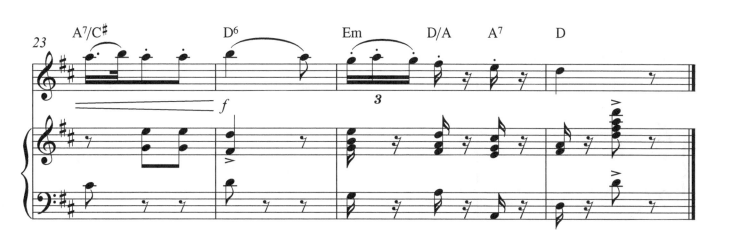

Allegro - la Primavera, RV. 269

Antonio Lucio Vivaldi

Menuett, BWV Anh 114

Johann Sebastian Bach

Allegretto

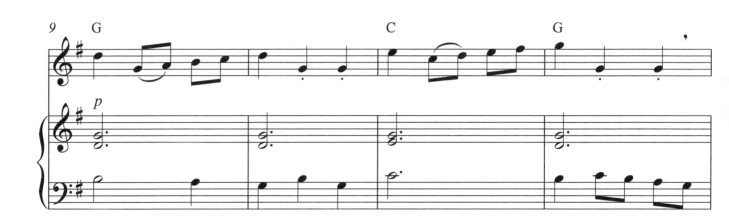

Ode an die Freude, Op. 125

Ludwig van Beethoven

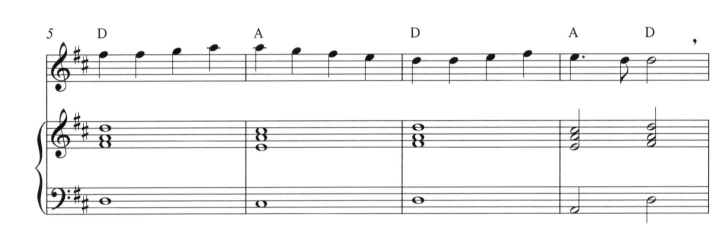
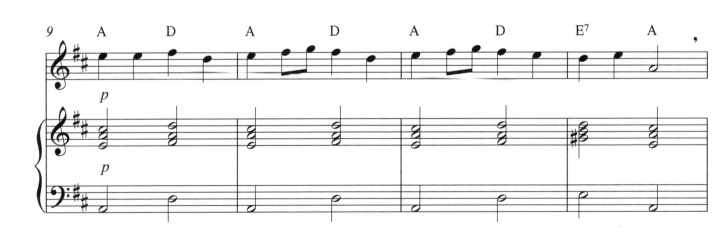

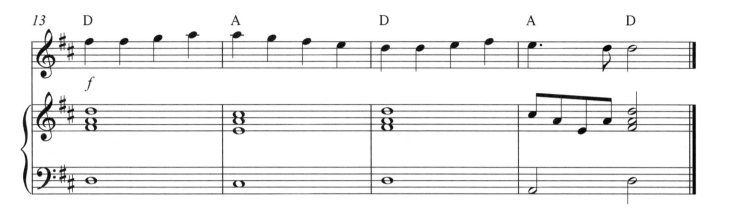

Pomp and Circumstance March Nº1, Op. 39

Edward Elgar

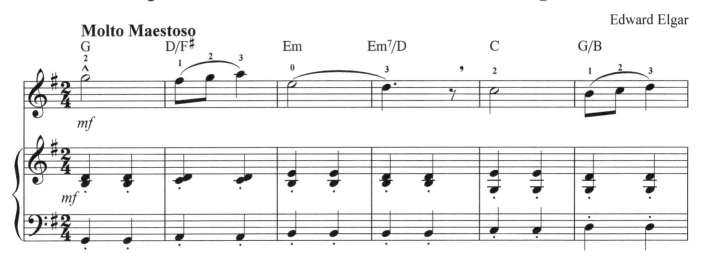
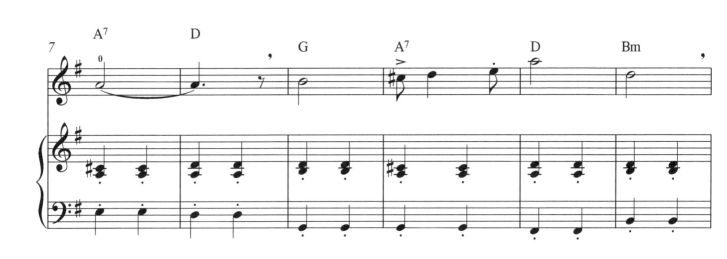
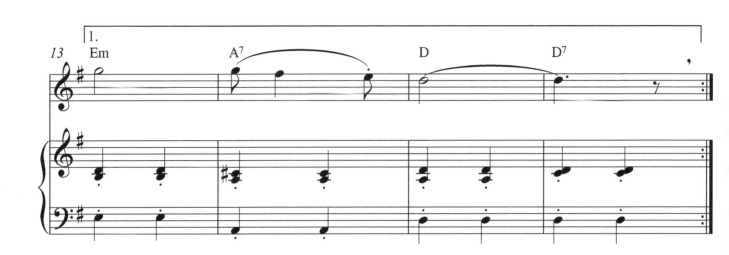

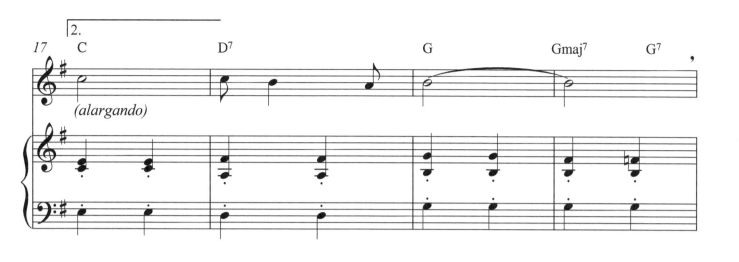
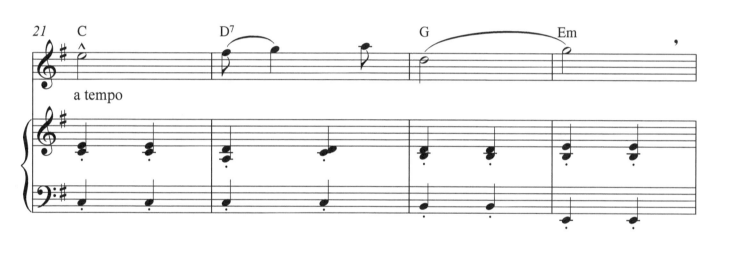
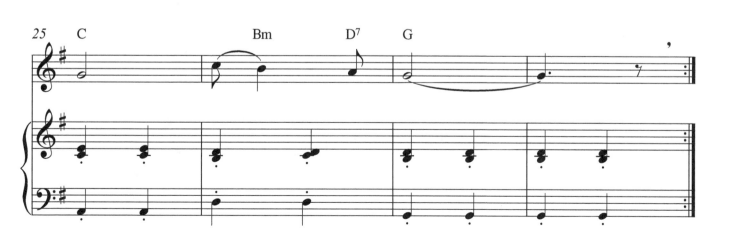

Treulich geführt

Richard Wagner

Molto Vivace

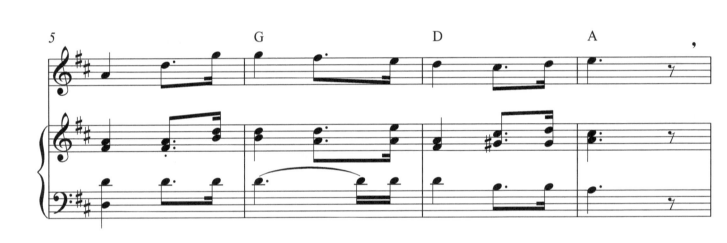
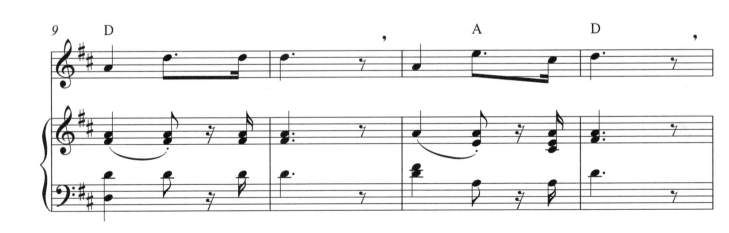

Alla Hornpipe - Water Music, HWV 349

George Frideric Handel

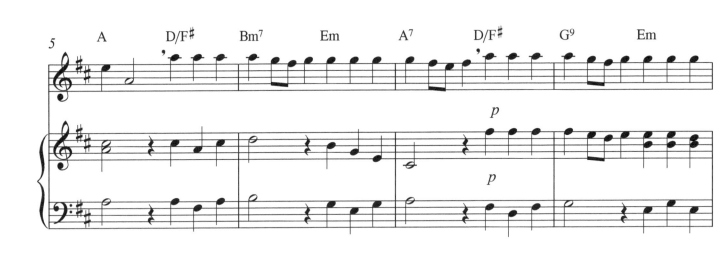

info@marcomusica.com

Made in United States
Troutdale, OR
11/21/2024

25142161R10031